Marie Van Brittan Brown
and Home Security

By Virginia Loh-Hagan

Published in the United States of America by
Cherry Lake Publishing
Ann Arbor, Michigan
www.cherrylakepublishing.com

Content Adviser: Kirsten Edwards, MA, Educational Studies
Reading Adviser: Marla Conn, MS, Ed., Literacy specialist, Read-Ability, Inc.

Photo Credits: © Don Pablo/Shutterstock.com, Cover, 1; © Jeff Whyte/Shutterstock.com, 4; ©Kheel Center/flickr.com, 6; © Grit_M02/Shutterstock.com, 8; © Spotmatik Ltd/Shutterstock.com, 10; © Dragon Images/Shutterstock.com, 12; ©Marie Van Brittan Brown (US3482037-0)/United States Patent and Trademark Office/www.uspto.gov, 14; © Kekyalyaynen/Shutterstock.com, 16; © nd3000 /Shutterstock.com, 18; © panuwat phimpha /Shutterstock.com, 20

Library of Congress Cataloging-in-Publication Data

Names: Loh-Hagan, Virginia, author.
Title: Marie van Brittan Brown and home security / by Virginia Loh-Hagan.
Description: Ann Arbor : Cherry Lake Publishing, [2018] | Series: Women innovators |
    Includes bibliographical references and index. | Audience: Grades 4 to 6.
Identifiers: LCCN 2018003302| ISBN 9781534129115 (hardcover) | ISBN 9781534132313 (pbk.) |
    ISBN 9781534130814 (pdf) | ISBN 9781534134010 (hosted ebook)
Subjects: LCSH: Brown, Marie van Brittan, 1922-1999—Juvenile literature. | African American inventors—Biography—Juvenile
    literature. | Women inventors—United States—Biography—Juvenile literature. | Electronic security systems—Juvenile literature. |
    Closed-circuit television—Juvenile literature.
Classification: LCC TH140.B743 L64 2018 | DDC 621.389/28092 [B] —dc23
LC record available at https://lccn.loc.gov/2018003302

Cherry Lake Publishing would like to acknowledge the work of The Partnership for 21st Century Skills.
Please visit *www.p21.org* for more information.

Printed in the United States of America
Corporate Graphics

CONTENTS

Criminals are sent to jail.

A Woman

Do you feel safe in your home? Do you feel safe in your neighborhood? Being safe means not being scared of getting hurt or being robbed. Some people do bad things. They break the law. They're **criminals**. They break into people's homes.

Police officers are community helpers. They try to keep people and neighborhoods safe. But they can't be everywhere. People

African Americans couldn't exercise
their right to vote until 1965.

have to take care of themselves. And that's what Marie Van Brittan Brown did.

Brown was a black female inventor. She invented the first home **security** system. She wanted to keep her family safe.

Life was not easy for Brown. She lived at a time when black people and women were not treated fairly.

She was born on October 30, 1922, in Queens, New York. She lived there until she died on February 2, 1999. She married Albert Brown and had two children. Her husband was an electronics **technician**.

Security systems watch what happens at a person's home.

Brown invented a video and **audio** security system. Her husband helped. She came up with the idea, and he built it. Together, they created an early model of a **closed-circuit** television system. In 1969, they got a **patent**.

Ask Questions!

Talk to a police officer. Ask about the safety of your neighborhood. Ask about the crime rate. Is your neighborhood safe or not? How can you make it safer?

Nurses work in hospitals. They help sick people.

An Idea

Brown was a nurse. She worked long hours. Her husband worked at night. Because of this, Brown and her children were home alone a lot.

Their neighborhood had a lot of crime. Police were slow to respond to emergency calls. She felt nervous whenever someone rang her doorbell. She wanted to be able to see and hear who was at her door from anywhere in her house.

Brown also used previous inventions like the television and the remote control in her design.

Like other inventors, Brown improved other designs. In the 1940s, a German engineer invented a camera system to observe rocket testing from a distance.

Brown took this idea and improved it so it could be used at home. This was a new idea. No one had thought of creating home **surveillance** systems.

Brown's invention had several **peepholes** and cameras on the door. The top peephole was for tall people, and the bottom one was for children. The cameras took images and sent them to a **monitor**.

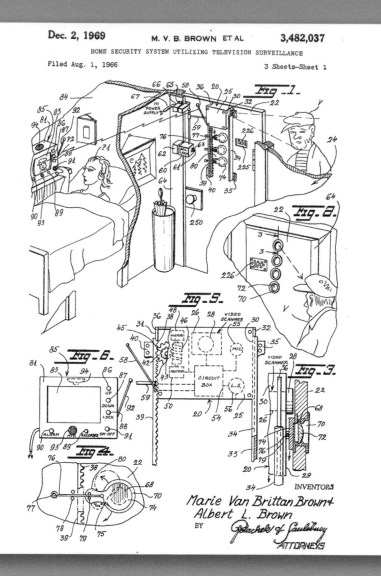

Brown wanted people to feel safe in their homes.

The monitor could be anywhere in the house.

The invention also had a microphone. It allowed people to speak to the person at the door. There was also a remote control that allowed people to unlock the door or call the police.

Create!

Create your own security system. Build on Brown's ideas. How can you improve on her invention?

Today, security systems are everywhere.

A Legacy

Brown didn't sell her idea. She didn't make any money. It would've been hard for a black woman to start a business. Most businesses were owned by white men.

Luckily, she filed a patent with her husband that gave her credit for her work. That wasn't easy to do, either. Not many black women could get patents at this time. But Brown did it. She was a role model for other black women inventors.

We may not know what Brown looks like, but we do know her invention keeps our houses safe.

She inspired other inventions. Her **legacy** can be seen in today's security systems. More than 10 inventors have used Brown's patent to build their own systems. Security systems using Brown's ideas can be found in houses, buildings, and offices.

Brown got some attention for her work. The National Scientists Committee gave her an award. Brown was also interviewed by the *New York Times*.

Today, millions of cameras are hidden in public places. People are being watched all

People today can monitor their homes from their tablets, smartphones, or laptops.

the time. This is to protect people and places. Security systems are all around us.

Brown's work is a part of our daily lives. But not many people know her name. There are few records of her life. But we are lucky to have her patent. Her ideas have kept us safe and secure.

Look!

Look all around you. Look for hidden cameras. Look for security systems. Why are they there? Do you feel safer? Do you think other people feel safer?

GLOSSARY

audio (AW-dee-oh) sound, especially when recorded, transmitted, or reproduced

closed-circuit (KLOHZD-SUR-kit) a system that uses video cameras to transmit images to a limited number of monitors

criminals (KRIM-uh-nuhlz) people who break the law

legacy (LEG-uh-see) something handed down from one generation to another

monitor (MAH-nih-tur) a screen that shows what is being recorded or transmitted

patent (PAT-uhnt) the right from the government to use or sell an invention for a certain number of years

peepholes (PEEP-hohlz) small holes to look through

security (sih-KYOOR-ih-tee) freedom from danger or risk

surveillance (sur-VAY-luhns) continuous observance of people or places

technician (tek-NISH-uhn) a person who has been trained to work with special equipment

FIND OUT MORE

BOOKS

Abdul-Jabbar, Kareem, and Raymond Obstfeld. *What Color Is My World? The Lost History of African-American Inventors*. Somerville, MA: Candlewick Press, 2012.

Lawrence, Sarah. *Anthology of Amazing Women: Trailblazers Who Dared to Be Different*. New York: Little Bee Books, 2018.

Sullivan, Otha Richard. *Black Stars: African American Women Scientists and Inventors*. San Francisco: Jossey-Bass, 2012.

WEBSITES

BlackPast.org—Marie Van Brittan Brown
www.blackpast.org/aah/brown-marie-van-brittan-1922-1999
Read a brief summary of Brown's life.

Medium—Timeline: This African American Woman Invented Your Home Security System
https://timeline.com/marie-van-brittan-brown-b63b72c415f0
Learn more about Brown and her invention.

INDEX

ABOUT THE AUTHOR

Dr. Virginia Loh-Hagan is an author, university professor, former classroom teacher, and curriculum designer. She has a video and audio surveillance system in her dogs' room. She lives in San Diego with her very tall husband and very naughty dogs. To learn more about her, visit www.virginialoh.com.